60 SECONDS TO

Shine

VOLUME 5

101 ORIGINAL ONE-MINUTE MONOLOGUES FOR WOMEN AGES 18–25
BY KRISTEN DABROWSKI

MONOLOGUE AUDITION SERIES

A Smith and Kraus Book

Published by Smith and Kraus, Inc.
177 Lyme Road, Hanover, NH 03755
www.SmithandKraus.com

First Edition: November 2007
10 9 8 7 6 5 4 3 2 1
Cover and text design by Julia Hill Gignoux

The Monologue Audition Series ISSN 1067-134X
ISBN 978-1-57525-572-9
Library of Congress Control Number 2007937053

CONTENTS

ACKNOWLEDGMENTS

To all the smart, sassy, fun, talented, and strong women
I've had the great fortune to know.

INTRODUCTION

Hello, actors! As a professional actor for fourteen years now, I know how hard the search for the perfect monologue can be. A monologue should be immediate, active, and fun. You shouldn't mind having to say it over and over when you're practicing, auditioning, or performing it. You should be able to relate to it. Often, you have very little time to make an impression. In those situations, your acting needs to be energetic, exciting, and natural. The purpose of this book is to make your auditions count!

Here are some tips on approaching monologues:

1) Pick the monologue that hits you. Trust your instincts. You'll pick the right one!

2) Make the monologues active. What do you want and how do you try to get it?

3) Who are you talking to and where are they? Make sure you make this as clear as possible.

4) Do you get answered or interrupted? Be sure to fill in words in your head for the moments when you are spoken to in the monologue, even if it's a simple "yes" or "no."

5) How do you feel about the person or people you are talking to? For example, you speak a lot differently to your best friend than you do to your math teacher.

6) Notes about stage directions and terminology: The word *beat* or the start of a new paragraph indicates another character speaks or a new idea arises. Stage directions like (*Shocked.*) are suggestions, but they do not need to be observed absolutely.

Break a leg!

Kristen Dabrowski

COMIC
MONOLOGUES

SIMPLE

comic

LORI

You're stressed out about the test? Why? This class is so easy. I don't know. I just think it makes total sense. All you have to do is talk in class sometimes and listen to the professor. He practically tells you the answers. Just listen to how he asks the questions and watch his face. Like last week, when he said, "Do you think slavery is the *only* reason for the Civil War?" his face was all scrunched up and he emphasized "only." So you know the answer is no. You just have to be observant. That's all.

You haven't been to class all semester? Well then, yeah. I guess you *do* have a problem.

LAUNDRY DAY

comic

AMANDA

Oh my God. Oh my God! I literally have no clean underwear! Oh, God, I really thought I had one more pair. Why didn't I do laundry yesterday? I even said that to you yesterday, do you remember? I was going to do laundry—what happened? Oh, yeah. I fell asleep. Oops. Listen, I know this is weird, but can I wear your underwear? I'll wash it. Or I'll buy you new ones! I promise.

Megan! I can't believe you won't do this for me! I'm desperate. I wouldn't ask you otherwise. I can't wear dirty underwear. That's disgusting. I'll buy you new ones . . . OK, fine! I'll just go commando. You are so dead to me.

BUILDING
comic

KAI

I had the most amazing experience today. The bookshelf that Dad ordered arrived today, right? So I took it into the den, and I put it together myself. I did! You can go and look. It was hard. The whole time I was thinking, "I can't do this. It's too heavy. It's too hard to do on my own." But I did it anyway. I tell you it seemed almost impossible. I'd be working on one side of it and the other side would collapse. I actually cried in the middle of it. But I kept going. I think it looks good. Go in and see it! I'm really proud of it.

It is not backwards!

MONKEY BOY
comic

OLIVIA

It must have been awful to be a woman in caveman times.
You'd just be so ugly. And all the guys would be ugly,
too. Do you think beauty standards were different then?
I guess they must have been. I just can't imagine how the
species didn't become extinct. Scott does not look like a
Neanderthal! You're crazy. I guess he does sort of have
a heavy brow, but—Oooo, I hate you, AnnMarie! You
ruined Scott for me forever! I'll never be able to look at
him the same again!

NOT OPRAH
comic

ANNABELLE

Oprah makes me sick. I guess she does great things, but sometimes . . . I just want to puke when rich people sit around talking about all they have. Yeah, she shouldn't have to lie about it, I suppose, and everyone knows she's rich . . . I don't know. I had to steal toilet paper from school yesterday. I'll admit it. My roommates and I don't have money to buy our own. It's pathetic, isn't it? I know! But that's how it is. So lately celebrities just make me sick.

Ugh, work? Why would I want to do that? Listen, making minimum wage isn't going to make me Oprah-rich. I'd rather steal toilet paper than work at the cafeteria.

THE PUPPY

comic

MYA

I look tired? I *am* tired! You know that adorable little puppy I got a few weeks ago? Well, he's not so cute anymore. He ate the leg off of the sofa. He pooped in my shoes. He ate my socks—somehow he managed to eat *one* of every pair I have! And he barks all night. I don't want him anymore. I mean it. I don't. I *can't* watch "The Dog Whisperer." Abercrombie ate through the TV cord. Nothing I own is sacred to him! I am at wits' end, Mollie. Normally, I would have put "puppy killer" at the very bottom of things I would be when I grow up. But now, I don't know . . .

I'm kidding! But I'm not. I swear, I hate that dog!

THE WAITING
comic

AYANA

I can't bear it any longer. The anticipation is killing me. God! I want this so bad. I cannot wait a second longer. Not even a millisecond. I'm going nuts.

(Starts to pace.) What am I waiting for? Why is there such a buildup to this? It's torture. I'm tingling all over. I think I might die. Now! Now! Now! Now!

I'm leaving. This is unbearable. Oh God!

It's my turn? I'm not ready; I'm not ready! OK, just a second. Coming! Mom, wish me luck on this audition!

LICENSE
comic

ALLI

I hate being late. And I'm powerless. I'm stuck in traffic! There's nothing I can do. There's probably an accident up ahead. I have no idea why people want to stop and stare at someone whose guts are on the sidewalk. It's sick. If it were me, I'd want people to look away. *(Shouting.)* If everyone would just put their foot on the gas pedal, we'd get there a lot faster! *(In a normal voice.)* I hate people, Cheryl. I swear, I do. Especially when I drive. No one can drive right! People don't signal. They slow down for no reason. They brake suddenly. They don't use common sense or pay attention. No one can drive, Cheryl!

(Gasps.) Oh! Whoops! I think I gotta go. I kinda bumped into the guy in front of me. Why can't anyone drive?

I LOVE SHOE

comic

MALLIKA

Yeah, he was cute, but did you see his shoes? They were like clown shoes. Not the size, the colors! I can't believe you didn't notice. They were so ugly.

Well, yeah, that's something I look at. *Everything's* important. I don't like to make mistakes, *especially* when it comes to guys. How they run, if they have a nice smile, if their voices are low or high—all of these things are important. Well, what do you look for?

Honesty? Sincerity? You are going to get yourself a real wimp that way. Don't you want a guy with some backbone? Well, yeah, there are personal qualities I look for. But if he has ugly shoes, who cares?

INTERVIEW

comic

ERIN

Do you mind if I stand? I know that's not usual, but when I'm nervous I like to stand. You should have seen me during the SATs! That was really hard for me, sitting all that time when I'm nervous. Am I the first person to stand during an interview here? Well, it makes me stand out, right? Am I making you nervous? I don't want to make you nervous just because I'm nervous. I can sit if you want. OK. *(Sits, but crosses legs and starts madly swinging her top leg.)* Is that better? I really want to go here. I do. This is my dream college. So I want this to go perfectly.

Relax? I am relaxed. This is me relaxed! OK. I'm lying, I'm not on crack of anything, but I think this is the best I can do at the moment!

ORDIN-MARY
comic

MARY

I was born in the wrong country. I'm supposed to be European. I'm sure of it. Being American is so boring. It's not exotic. Whatever, Dad. I guess it *could* be exotic to someone from, I don't know, Siberia, but that's about it. American culture is everywhere. There's no mystery to it. And it's so . . . We have cowboys and plantations. That's about as exotic as it gets. There's no glamour to that. The South is where the slaves were, so that's not that cool. And the West is so . . . dirty. I'm not saying you have to agree with me, but that's how I see it. Why can't we be Spanish or Moroccan or something like that? I am just doomed to be ordinary. I mean, we live in Connecticut! It couldn't get any less exotic!

SO HOT
comic

NATALIE

I hate being sick. I cannot stop sneezing. I'm sorry. I have to blow my nose. *(Blows her nose.)* Sorry. If I got up from the table every time I had to blow my nose, I'd never get to eat!

Look, I'm not contagious. I've had this cold for weeks now. So, you wanna make out after this? I don't feel like going to a movie. Everyone in the theater will be mad at me for coughing and sneezing every two minutes.

No? Why not? Don't you think I'm pretty? Hold on a sec. *(Blows nose again.)* So what's your problem?

SEXED OUT
comic

HANNAH

Sex, sex, sex, sex, sex! Everywhere I look—sex! I actually think I'm getting bored of it. I'm over it. I think I am. It's official. I'm going to just watch Disney movies and cartoons from now on. If I so much as see Paris Hilton, I'm going to close my eyes and cover my ears and sing "Yankee Doodle." We are all way too preoccupied with something that is basically, when you think about it, a really strange thing that's meant to bring new babies into the world. When you think about it that way, it's amazing anyone thinks about it at all. I am going to go a whole week without thinking or seeing anything about sex. I will! I bet it will make me a better person. Maybe even more creative or something. I just think we need a new topic.

I don't know what we'd talk about otherwise, that's the whole point! But I'm going to find out.

RE-ROUTE

comic

SOPHIA

No. I don't want to even walk past where I work. I'd
rather starve than walk by the food court. I just don't
want to be reminded. I have to go back there soon—See,
you made me think about it! I just want to have one
whole day where I don't think about it. One whole day
when I can imagine that I'm free, without a care in the
world. Let me live that fantasy, Lindsey! Don't burst my
bubble. For one day, I want to imagine I'm a rich girl
who doesn't work at Fat Wok every day after classes. Is
that too much to ask? Listen, if you wait to eat, I'll buy
you dinner on the way home tonight. Sure, it will blow all
my pathetic earnings for the week, but the fantasy will go
on. Besides, there's always the dollar menu, right?

HUNGRY
comic

RAISA

I'm so hungry. My stomach is burning. Mom, when are we going to eat? You said we'd eat at six. It's six-thirty! Can I make myself a sandwich? You said it would be ready "any minute" ten minutes ago! I've been hungry for hours now.

I'm not whining! I'm just telling you how I feel. I even offered to make my own meal. I'd say I'm being pretty terrific right now. Oh no. You're kidding, right? You can't send me to my room without dinner! I'm not being bratty! I'm just really, really hungry, Mom. Please, are we eating soon?

DISTRACTION
comic

JENNIFER

Stop doing that paper. Stop it! I'm bored. I need to be en-
tertained. Why are you working so hard? You've been
doing that same paper for days. I just write my papers
once, right before class. It works out fine. My grades are
good. I bet they're as good as yours. Or at least almost as
good. It's not worth it to spend, like, eighty extra hours
doing a paper just to get an A instead of a B+. At least
come to dinner with me. I hate going to the dining hall
alone! It's the worst. Looking around for anyone you
know to eat with? It's pathetic. And it's the absolute
worst when you don't see *anyone* you know, and you end
up asking some random girl you recognize from your history class if you can sit with her and her friends. Come
on, Heidi. The paper can wait. It's not going to get better.
I bet it's perfect now! Come ooooonnnnnnnnnn . . .

Oh my God, you've left me with an impossible choice. Sit
around here with you, starving and bored out of my
skull, or go do the lonely walk through the cafeteria,
holding a tray of mystery meat and stringy string beans.
You're a vicious bitch, you know that?

BONDING

comic

LYNN

Grandma, can you explain Bingo to me? I understand it,
I just don't get why you go. Have you ever won a lot of
money or anything? Then what's the point?

It's social? But aren't you just listening to the guy calling
out the numbers and stamping a card? You're not chat-
ting to your friends are you? Huh. What else do you do
for fun? Well, that's pretty much what I do. Yeah! My
friends and I just sit around and talk all the time. I guess
things haven't changed so much.

So, one more question. I hope you don't mind. I like to
know about you. Do you . . . have any teeth still?

BRAVE

comic

TRACY

You can't do this! You've got to be kidding. Being naked in front of other people? Part of me is amazed at your bravery. The other part of me thinks you're nuts! People will see you. People from here! From college! College guys will be looking at you naked.

I know you need money for next term. But isn't there another way? I'm sure you'll make more money being naked than working in the library. But, Serena, . . . being an artists' model? People will see you naked from all directions! There will be a record of your nakedness for all time! *I* could never do it. That's all I know.

BIG NIGHT
comic

NIKKI

Joe is coming tonight. I'm cooking him dinner. It seemed like a good idea. We've been together for a year, I finally have my own apartment—it seemed like a good idea.

Why did it seem like a good idea?! Right now, it seems like such a *bad* idea. An awful idea. I can't cook! I make grilled cheese and mac and cheese and things with cheese! That's it! I buy things in boxes and put them in the microwave! He's going to expect a romantic, homemade meal, and I am going to give him chicken nuggets and Tater Tots. I know, everyone does love Tater Tots! But that will not do for this meal!

No, forget it. I'm calling him to cancel. I'm just not ready yet. This is too big a step.

SMOKED
comic

CANDY

Can I tell you how stupid I am? Shane asked me to go running with him. He runs every morning. Of course, I said yes since I've been flirting with him for months now. So, we meet. We start running. It's all very pleasant. We're talking and running. But, as you know, I am out of shape, and after only a few minutes, I'm gasping for breath. I keep going. I want to impress. I feel like I have to pee from all the up and down pounding against the sidewalk. I feel like I have to vomit because I'm so out of shape. I want a cigarette more than life itself.

So, long story short, I vomit and pee myself. I'm totally humiliated. So, to deal with my stress, I pull out a cigarette, light up, and find the courage to look Shane in the eye. And he says to me, "I could never go out with a smoker." I mean, I vomited and peed myself and smoking is the problem?

ADMISSION
comic

KEENA

I'm smiling? I guess I'm happy. I don't know. I'm happy to be here with you. This is fun! You're having fun, too? You know, Robert . . . I like you. I really do. I guess I'm trying to say that I—You like me, too? Really? Like you *like* me?

Isn't this bizarre? We're talking like we're kids. I'm so embarrassed! Am I turning red? I've just never gotten good at this. But I'm so glad you like me, too. I mean, you mean you like me as a girlfriend, right? Oh. I'm so relieved! For a second . . . I really like you, Robert. I do.

THE JOB
comic

CAITLIN

Should I wear a suit? Do people still do that? I want to make a good impression, to show that I take this seriously. But I don't want to seem snobby. I don't want to be so dressed that the other employees think I'm an ice queen. But if I dress down too much, maybe my boss will think I can't move up and do more important things. I want to climb the ladder as fast as possible. Get more money, a better job.

OK, breathe. This is going to be fine. It's just one day. Just one first day of work ever at a real job. Not a big deal. Millions of other people are probably doing the same thing right now. Oh, my God, I've been talking so long—I'm late!

GENETICS
comic

KIT

I always thought my mother and I were really different.
We have different personalities, different ways of thinking, different senses of humor—but today, I had the most
shocking realization. I have my mother's hips! I've gained
some weight over the last few years, and I'm not skinny
anymore. It's horrifying. I used to be able to eat anything.
I hated how my mom was always on a diet. But it snuck
up on me. I don't even know exactly when it happened. I
never, *never* thought I'd have my mom's body. She used to
say that she was thin when she was younger—I thought
she was full of crap!

If I ever start nagging you to clean your room, Nancy, I
want you to do an intervention. There's no way I can become my mother. I can't believe I'm saying this, but I am
joining a gym today!

TRICKED
comic

ELLEN

Excuse me. This smoothie is twenty-seven *hundred* calories? It has fruit in it! It's supposed to be good for you. Isn't that your whole angle—that your smoothies are healthy? So what the hell in here is making this so many calories? I feel so cheated. I'm never coming back. Except that I'm addicted to these stupid smoothies now. I *have* to come back. This is just like tobacco, you know! You got me addicted on these things before I knew they were dangerous. I could sue you. I could make millions.

Oh my God. I just feel so betrayed. I mean, I know this isn't *your* fault, you just work here, but this company has completely destroyed my life. I hate you guys so much!

DECISIONS
comic

CAROLINE

Yeah, I like vanilla. What's wrong with that? It's boring? Why? You're looking at me like you think my ice cream choice is a reflection on my personality. Whatever you think of vanilla, *I'm* not boring. You are making way too much of this! I can't believe you're being so weird! No, I don't like Chunky Monkey. I don't like extra stuff in my ice cream. No, not even chocolate chips.

Is this a problem? You really shouldn't read so much into little things.

So, how many pairs of pants do you own? I always see you in the same jeans. That's it? Just the one pair? Oh my God, I'm seeing you in a whole new light now.

HEALTH HAZARD
comic

AMY

Oh my gawd, Crystal, there is the biggest damn roach in the world in here! What are we gonna do? I am never eating here again. I don't care. I'm going to the Burger King down the street on my break. Maybe they have roaches, too, but as long as I don't know it, I don't care. This place is such a hole. I can't believe I work here!

I can't hold back. I'm sorry, but this is too freakin' nasty. I'm gonna scream. I don't care if the manager is on the floor. This is too disgusting. Ah! It's coming for me! Oh my gawd, Crystal, kill it! Kill it! *(Jumping on a chair. Screaming.)* This restaurant has roaches! I am outta here! I'll mail back my uniform!

WHOLE NEW LIFE
comic

GINA

This isn't right. It doesn't give off the right message. This says, "I'm prim and proper." It's too *good*. It's too work-place. I need something that says I'm hip, I'm fun, I'm a party person. Something relaxed but trendy. Something that says that I'm the kind of person who gets text messages every other minute. It should say, "I'm here" but not "Look at me." Know what I mean? Yeah, it has to say a lot. In fact, it should even speak French. And maybe Spanish, too. A little sophistication with a dash of salsa. This is important, Renee, focus! I just don't have anything like that. This is a moment. I have an opportunity to rethink myself, to remake myself, to be a whole new person! This isn't something to be taken lightly. We are new to this place. No one knows us. No one knows who we used to be. And this is our first party. We have a chance to make a whole new impression and get a new life, Renee. We can get a life in general! Our closets are hopeless. We have to get to the mall.

To the car!

MATCH

comic

GLORIA

I like you. I do. We matched up perfectly, didn't we? So our personalities must mesh. But here's the thing. There are twenty-four other people who matched up with me. I think I at least owe them the opportunity of meeting me, and vice versa. You should do the same! You might meet someone who's even more compatible. It's too soon to limit ourselves!

I'm looking for a soul mate, too, Ryan. There's, like, one soul mate for everyone. One! Not twenty-five. So I have to meet all of you. Look, this is a lot of pressure for a first date. I really think you need to cool down. I had a lot of fun tonight, but I don't think it's time to register for wedding gifts yet. I know you're just asking for a second date, but this is moving too fast for me. Why don't I just e-mail you when I'm ready to move forward, OK?

HIS PLACE

comic

VALERIE

This place does not come clean. Do you ever clean? Have you ever cleaned? Don't lie. Look me in the eye when you say that.

Well then why is this place such a sty? I'm your girlfriend, not your maid. I should not have to clean your apartment. *You* should clean it, so I want to stay here. You don't want me to stay here? Oh, that's just beautiful. Nice. Very nice. Is that some kind of joke? Do you think you're so hot, you're such an eligible bachelor, Mr. Sexiest Man Alive, that you can take me for granted? That you can do better? Well, good luck. You will never find a woman alive who is as sexy and gorgeous as me who will also clean your tub. And I can cook, too. You think about that. If you come to your senses, do a thorough clean—*thorough*, like white glove—and call me. 'Til then, have a nice life, Bryan.

GALLERY OPENING
comic

HEATHER

Excuse me. What gives you the right to judge me exactly? Were you ever an artist yourself? No. You're just some guy who came here and wants to feel superior. Did it ever occur to you that you don't know what you're talking about? That you wouldn't know good art if it fell on you?

Yes, this is my work! I went to art school. *I* studied. This is a brilliant sculpture. Look at the play between positive and negative space. It took me weeks to get this looking exactly how I wanted it. Before you start making judgments, maybe you should get some information. Think, research before you speak.

From *The Times*? Art review? So . . . you . . . didn't like it . . . sir? My God, I didn't notice 'til just this minute how handsome you are!

YOGA CLASS

comic

SONYA

No. I can't go back. I had an . . . incident at yoga class. So I can't go back. Ever. I really can't. Won't.

It's no use asking, Jeanette! I can't talk about it. Let's just say it was embarrassing. Something embarrassing. How did you know? It was awful! The whole room was completely silent and then—I farted. Big time. I didn't even know it was coming. And there was no use trying to pretend it was someone else. It was so obvious. So, clearly, I can't go back there. I may never do yoga again. At least in an aerobics class the music is loud.

Jeanette, it does not happen to everyone! I mean it smelled! I'm not going back and that's that.

HEAVY PETTING
comic

CARLENE

You got a dog? Are you kidding? Why didn't you consult me? I know I've been at college, but that doesn't mean I shouldn't be consulted. I do come back here during breaks. So that means that I have to deal with this damn dog, too! Couldn't you just wait until I move out?

What am I so upset about? I'm treated like I'm not part of this family—out of sight, out of mind, I guess! Not to mention dog hair, dog breath, dog smell, dog poop—need I go on? Barking! Dogs are disgusting, and I don't want one.

Oh my God, he's so little! Oh, Mommy, I love him!

R.I.P.

comic

BABS

Noooooo! Look! My jeans! My favorite jeans! They died!
I knew I shouldn't have washed them. The rip in the
crotch met up with the rip in the knee. Can you sew? Can
they be saved? Well, it's not exactly on the seam . . . Oh,
I'll never find another another pair like you, Old Blue!
You served me so well. We went everywhere together. Remember the ninth grade dance where we danced with
Kevin O'Brien? Yeah, I've had these since ninth grade! I
loooove these jeans. We've done everything together. This
is really sad. I actually think I might cry.

Ellie, let's bury them tonight. Have a funeral. Yes, I'm serious! Old Blue deserves a funeral. Don't laugh! Don't listen to her, Blue. She doesn't understand you like I do.

THE DAY AFTER
comic

MARKI

Shhhh! Stop shouting! Be quiet. I need quiet. I drank *way* too much yesterday. I feel like death. There's no way I can make class today. Why did I start on the shots? That's what really did me in. When did we get home?

Matt did shots off my stomach? Stop. That is not funny. I feel sick. No. That can't be true. I wouldn't do that.

Well, yeah, I was trying to make Steve jealous, but Matt? He's so . . . yucky. No, no. Don't even mention food. I need coffee. And don't tell me anything more about last night or I will definitely puke.

STUDYING
comic

NELL

We weren't doing anything! The door was closed because we needed to concentrate. We're *studying*. I *told* you we were studying. What are you thinking? Get your mind out of the gutter, Dad. Give me a little credit. Do you really think I'd be up here having sex while you're in the kitchen? That would be too weird for words. And I'm not like that. In case you haven't noticed, I'm a straight-A student. I do that by studying, which is what I'm doing now with Tommy. *Studying*, Dad.

Can you shut the door on the way out? We need to concentrate. Really. We have a *physics* test.

Where were we, Tommy, before we were so rudely interrupted? Ah yes. You were kissing my neck.

COMPROMISE
comic

B.J.

Beer cans in a pyramid do not a decorating scheme make. You can't keep them! Why would you want to? What's so special about beer cans? So what they're from your twenty-first birthday party? They're *beer cans*. We're *married*. We need to compromise. So you need to get rid of those beer cans. I am not going to live in an apartment with beer cans piled in the middle of the living room! David! Be serious! You're not a kid anymore! And you don't live alone. You have to take me into consideration. They have to go!

No, I am not going to give up my teddy bears! I've had them since I was a little girl. You only had your beer cans since you were twenty-one. Besides, my teddies are not in the *living room* for all to see. And they're not ugly! David, you have to compromise! Now!

BIG DAY
comic

TANYA

Daylight Savings Time? So what time is it now? Oh my God. No. No. No-no-no-no-no! Why didn't you wake me? You wanted to let me sleep? Why? That was not being nice! That was being stupid! How could you be so thoughtless? I have a presentation, and I overslept! Oh God! Oh Lord! Oh holy—Where are my socks? Where are my shoes? Where are my keys? I can't shower. I have no time to shower. I can't believe I have no time to shower! This is a disaster. I smell—I smell! Don't I? Do I? Oh, God, I'm screwed!

Let go of me! I have to get out of the door now! What? What? It's—what? Sunday? No, yesterday was Sunday. Today is Monday. Wait—what? It's . . . Sunday. It's Sunday! Holy hell that scared me. My heart is beating a mile a minute. I gotta go back to bed.

PACKING

comic

KARYN

It won't fit! I can't leave this country. My suitcase will not close. No matter what I do! I sat on it. I rearranged it. I rolled everything. It just will not close! I can't leave anything. Are you nuts? There's no time to buy another bag. We have to leave for the airport in an hour! Do you have any more space? Why did the exchange rate have to be so good? I couldn't resist! Besides, you can't find any things this good in the Gap or whatever. I was helping the world economy!

What can I do? I guess I can leave my book for the plane. And—what else? Everything else is essential! Oh, I give up. I'll leave my underwear. It's all I can spare! Can you imagine what the next person coming into this room will think when they find a drawer full of panties and bras?

NOSH

comic

MEREDITH

You've got to help me. Make me stop. I have a bagel with cream cheese every morning, and it is making me fat, fat, fat. But I love them. If I don't have my bagel with cream cheese and coffee every morning I'm just miserable. I've tried having other things, better things, like eggs or even a salad or oatmeal, but it just doesn't *do* it. And if I'm being totally honest here, I have a bagel with cream cheese for lunch a lot, too. It's fast! And easy! I don't always have a lot of time for lunch. How many cups of coffee have I had? Four so far. I need coffee to keep me going. I lead a busy life. I'm always running late. I have no time. So a bagel and coffee are the best choice for me. Well, I'm thinking about this because I'm taking this health class, and the teacher pretty much told me that I'm killing myself, and I'm a huge slob. Part of me is like eeeek! And the other part of me is like, well, I'd rather die happy than hungry. And I don't know which part to listen to!

I need another cup of coffee so I can figure this out.

PERFECT

comic

ZANDRA

I'm terrified that he's a serial killer or something. He's just so nice and perfect. He's always considerate. He holds the door for me. He told me that I have the nicest eyes. Isn't that sweet? There's just got to be something wrong with him, though. He can't be *perfect*, right? He even brought me flowers on our first date! Perfect, right? Since he's so right, I can't help thinking there's got to be something wrong with him. Really wrong. Someone can't be this good, right? He did say, though, that he has lots of sisters, and he gets along with his mom, and he was a geek in school. He's not now, though! He's really cute. But maybe that accounts for why he's so nice.

Is it possible that he's just a great guy? I suppose so. It could be. There might be a perfect guy in the world right now. And that this guy is really into me. It's possible that I could meet this guy while I'm still really young, and we could be happy together for the rest of our lives. But, seriously, Monica, how likely is that?

SERIOUS
comic

SIENNA

Do I want to have children? I think I'm a little young to even think about that. I don't know. I'm a freshman in college. I guess maybe. Then again, maybe a baby won't fit into my life. Maybe I'll never get married. I don't want to have a baby if I'm not married. Maybe if I were very rich, but if I'm not, it's too hard to raise a baby on your own. How about you?

Ten. You want ten kids. Ten. You want to find a woman who will spend a decade pregnant. Do you have any idea how hard that would be on a woman's body? Ten kids!

No, I wouldn't consider that. Where are you going? Are you serious? It's our first date in the first week of college, and you're walking away from me (quite rudely, I might add) because I don't think that someday I'll want to have ten kids? You are nuts!

VALENTINE'S DAY
comic

DREW

You're not making a plan. There's no plan. So—what? We're going to have pizza on Valentine's Day? See a movie? No. I don't think so. I don't think that's what we're going to do because that's what we always do. Well, that is, when we get out of your room where you sit day and night playing *video games* like a third grader. No, on Valentine's Day you are going to do something special. You should be writing this down! Take some notes. I mean it. Get a pen. For Valentine's Day, you will make a reservation at a nice restaurant (and we will not split the bill), you will come to my door with flowers and candy, and you will bring me a special present. Something that shows how much I mean to you. I've been dropping hints for three weeks, Tim. Think about it. I can't do everything for you. Oh, and you will dress nice. Like a suit. No, I'm not kidding! Do you want me to wear a nice dress? Let me put it this way: cleavage. OK? Are we on the same page now? You'd better not screw this up, Tim.

THE ESSAY
comic

JENNIFER

This is so hard. Do I want to try to tell them what they want to hear or what I really think? What *do* they want to hear? And what *do* I think? I haven't a clue about either. That's what college is for, right? For me to figure things out. Should I go way out on a limb and say something no one's ever said before? Like what? I don't know what. Maybe that I'd like to be the first botanist on Mars or something. Or that out of everyone, dead or alive, I'd most like to have dinner with the guy who invented wheat germ because why did he invent wheat germ? It boggles my mind that way back when people would just taste things that looked inedible. What made him think wheat germ would be a big seller? Did he ever taste it himself? Was he "regular"?

OK. The wheat germ thing is out, even though I do think about that. So what is the one, exact, right thing to say that will get me in?

SHOVELING
comic

GRETCHEN

Oh, hi. It's been a while. How are you? I'm fine. Yeah. What do I do? I work at a zoo. Yeah. It's fun. I've always loved animals. You look great. Really glamorous and successful. What do you do? Oh, wow. I don't even know what that is exactly. Hedge funds. I know it's not about bushes and landscaping, but that's where my knowledge ends.

At the zoo? Oh, well, I work in the, uh, maintenance area. Make sure all the animals are comfortable. You know, I—I shovel. You know, the cages. The waste. Yeah. I'm sorry, I probably smell awful now. I do love animals, and there's a lot of opportunity to move up, but this is where you kind of have to start at the zoo. There are actually a lot of people who want to do this kind of work. It's actually pretty competitive. Not like hedge funds, probably, but it's good. I'm hoping to get moved up to the monkey house soon. It's exciting. Yeah.

SERIOCOMIC
MONOLOGUES

THE STUDENT/TEACHER
seriocomic

GRACIELLA

That teacher is a complete bitch. I can't stand her! I was sick on Wednesday. I *couldn't* come to class. So why can't I make up that quiz? She is just trying to mess up my grade. I bet she's enjoying herself. How do teachers get like that? I would never turn into a total bitch. I would be so nice. I swear.

Well, of course I'd be respected! Why wouldn't I be? You know what, I don't even care about that. I'd rather just be cool. Be the teacher I wish I had!

THE BODY
seriocomic

MARIA

Where I come from this body looks good. If I showed up home looking like a bony white girl (no offense), my whole family—no, my whole neighborhood—would freak. My mom would want to feed you. I'm not kidding. She would sit you down immediately and put as much food in front of you as she could lay her hands on.

It's not just women! No, it's the men, too. They like a little something to grab onto. You think I'm kidding. You have to go home with me. It will change your world. I *guarantee* that all the guys in the neighborhood will be whistling at *me*, and they probably won't even notice you. Don't get me wrong, you're pretty, but there is nothing wrong with having some curves, girl!

ALTERATIONS

seriocomic

KATE

Mom, I don't want to get my teeth fixed. I think that space is cute! Come on, it will save you loads of money if I don't. I won't be sorry when I older! I like my teeth. I don't want to look like everyone else.

If you really want to spend money on me, I could use, um, implants. I'm really flat! And that's something that does kind of bother me. I don't care about my teeth!

Why is getting my teeth fixed a good thing, but getting my boobs fixed a bad thing? It doesn't make sense to me! This is so unfair. I don't understand you! My body is my own; I should get to do what I want with it!

PICKY
seriocomic

JOYCE

I don't eat corn. I'm sorry, Mrs. Logan. No, I don't like
string beans either. I'm not a vegetable person. Yeah. My
dad jokes that I eat like a man. I like steak and potatoes;
I admit it! You're a vegetarian? Oh. Well. Sorry. Did I of-
fend you? I didn't mean to. I mean, I've seen Jeremy eat
meat, I think. No? I could have sworn . . . You know,
when I think about it, I realize we always eat pizza, don't
we? Isn't it strange that I never noticed you're a vegetarian? Wow. So . . . what do you eat for Thanksgiving
then? Tofurky? Oh. Great.

It's fine. Really. No, I'm not crying. I'm just . . . surprised,
that's all.

FRIDAY NIGHT
seriocomic

LUCY

Could you stop that? I'm trying to study. You don't even know me! How do you know I need to "lighten up"? Maybe you should stop being a lazy slob. Look, you made a judgment about me first. Could you please not play football in the hall? There's a huge quad outside— why don't you play there? I can't even tell you how many times I've heard you guys out here and just kept my mouth shut because I didn't want to make waves. But, honestly, grow up. This is college. To me, college is a way to get a good job and a good life, not a place to act like a four-year-old. I mean, really! Would you vomit in the hallways and throw ice cream into the heating vents at home?

Oh, forget it. I'll go to the library. You're idiots.

MISSING
seriocomic

REAGAN

Where is my phone? Have you seen—oh my God, where
is it? My whole life is in that phone! If I miss a call—I
can't buy a new one! Help me look. Don't just sit there!
This is an emergency; I can't calm down. Stop criticizing
me! I do not always lose things! Look, your negativity is
not helping! My whole life is in that phone, Nick!

Oh my Lord, thank you, thank you! You saved my life!
You had it the whole time? Idiot! You think that's funny?
That is the sickest joke ever. You are not funny.

HOMEWORK HELL
seriocomic

LILIANA

There are not enough hours in the day to do all my homework. Why don't the teachers get together and talk about this? How am I supposed to write a paper for English class, three chapters in history, do a page of math problems, and hand in a lab analysis all in one day? It's not humanly possible! No wonder people cheat. There's no choice! Teresa, I'll do the English and math if you'll do the science and history. Oh, I forgot all about French! I hate French. What's the point? Everyone speaks English anyway. Is college worse than this? Well, at least there's no gym class. I could almost bear all this pressure if I didn't have to run a mile after lunch every day.

SENTIMENTAL
seriocomic

FAYE

Ooo, Mom, noooo! I love that couch! I grew up on that couch! You can't get rid of it. You're just going to throw it out? Why? We don't need a new one. *You* see it as falling apart, *I* see it as broken in. In a good way! Like a pair of jeans. It's perfect now. Perfectly comfortable! Pleeeeease don't throw it out, Mom. I love it! I know I'm sentimental, but it's one of the only things left from my childhood. I sit on the couch when I'm sick and watch TV, I jumped up and down on it with John when we were little, we'd make the cushions into a fort—this couch has memories!

Can it go in my room then? Pleeeeease! Have a heart!

HELPFUL
seriocomic

EVA

I had the most horrifying realization today. My life is in a tailspin now. You know I've wanted to be an emergency-room doctor my whole life. My whole, entire life! I've never, ever wanted to be anything else. And now that this has happened . . . You didn't hear? I can't believe it hasn't made the rounds yet! It's so humiliating. Laura Mannis hit Lisa Shapelli in the head with her hockey stick. And Lisa's head—Hold on. I need to breathe. Relax. OK. So, Lisa's head is bleeding. Like a dummy, I pass out. Cold! Fainted dead away. In front of everyone. Me. The emergency-room doctor. A person who watches surgery on TV every chance I get. This changes my whole life! Not only is it humiliating—

You're not just saying that, are you? That happens to med students? Are you *sure*? God, I hope you're right. I really, really hope so!

RUINED

seriocomic

JULIE

(Screams.) I can't believe I just did that. Where is it? *(Falls to the floor and mimes scrambling about, looking for something.)* Do you see where it went, Kate? Oh! I got it! *(Stands.)* It's not working. Oh my God. It's not working! I *just* got this iPod for Christmas—my parents are going to *kill* me. It has to work. There has to be a way to fix it.

Look for yourself. The screen is blank. I'm not stupid. It doesn't work. I'm not being rude. I'm panicked. You would be, too. This is major. I have the worst luck in the world!

SICK
seriocomic

HOLLY

Uhhh, could we pull over, Mr. Wills? I wouldn't ask,
but—Can we please pull over now? It's an emergency. I'm
sorry. I'm—going to puke. I'm sorry. *(Stands. Takes a few
steps forward. Breathes deeply.)* I think I just need some
fresh air. I feel a little better. Everyone is staring at me.
(Breathes deeply again.) I cannot throw up. I'm sorry. I
just need a minute, Mrs. Peterson. I just felt sick. I get
carsick sometimes. This was such a long trip, and with
the bus being so stuffy . . . Just give me a minute. I'm
sorry.

Could you maybe tell everyone to stop staring at me? It's
not helping.

FUNNY GIRL

seriocomic

SARAH

You know, everyone says they like me. Some random girl at a store last week told me I had a really fun personality. Really! I don't know, I was just asking her about whether this T-shirt was on sale. But we're getting off the topic. How come if everyone likes me, no one *likes* me, you know? I'm not anyone's best friend, and I'm not anyone's girlfriend. I'm sort of separate. It's like everyone comes to me when they want a joke, but that's it. No one confides in me, no one flirts with me—I'm a *buddy* to guys. Do you know how annoying that is?

I don't want to be some dumb bimbo wearing tiny shirts and batting my eyelashes at them. I don't think I should have to be. Why can't I get noticed for being *me*? I guess I don't understand how all this works. I know I'm not your best friend like Jenna is, but I could really use some help. What am I doing wrong?

VINTAGE
seriocomic

EDEN

What's wrong? Yeah, I shop here. I find a lot of cute
stuff. And it's so cheap. Last week, I got a shirt here for a
dollar. Of course someone else owned it! That's how thrift
stores work. You recycle cans, right? Well, this is recy-
cling clothes. It's good for the environment. Don't you
give your old clothes to the poor? Well, I'm not *poor*, but
I'm poor, if that makes sense. Well, I have no money of
my own, really. Besides, I don't know what you're getting
so weird about. First of all, I *wash* the clothes after I take
them home. Second of all, you've told me a bunch of
times that you like things I've bought here! You have!

God, you're so superficial. Fine, we'll go to the mall after
this.

I DARE YOU
seriocomic

VICKY

Do you think this theater is really haunted? It seems too new to be haunted. That's just the kind of thing people say to freak each other out. I don't believe it.

No, I'm not going to come here at night. Why would I? That's stupid. I don't have to prove myself to you. We're not seven anymore. I don't take dares! Seriously, Mike, don't be a baby. *I'm* a baby? *I'm* a baby. That is just funny. Fine. Fine! I'll come and sleep here tonight. You'd better help me carry my stuff over here. If I'm going to sleep on the floor at least I'd better be comfortable. Are you going to do it, too? Why not? Scared, baby? I dare you to stay here in this haunted theater all alone in the dark with me tonight.

COLD
seriocomic

AMARISA

I'm so cold. I can't believe I forgot my gloves this morning! This is unbearable. It must be twenty below out here!

Oh. That's nice of you to . . . hold my hands. I *am* cold. But, I have to say this is a little awkward. You don't *like* me, do you? Because I have a boyfriend. Yeah, we've been together a long time. I can't believe you didn't know that. No, it's OK. You didn't know. Don't worry about it. I'm really not that cold anyway. My hands will be fine. You know, I'm sick of waiting for the bus. Maybe I'll just walk to class.

LOUD
seriocomic

KELLY ANN

Loud? You think I'm loud? I bet if one of your buddies acted just like me you'd think nothing of it. Guys are such jerks. If a female is strong and assertive, you're too loud, too bossy—

What are you doing? Are you putting your fingers in your ears? That's so rude! That's the rudest thing anyone has ever done in my presence. What's that? Your hearing aid? You have hearing problems?

Oh. Your hearing aid was up too high. I never noticed— your hair is kind of long. I feel—I'm so sorry. I—Do you hate me now?

ADVISOR

seriocomic

VERONICA

Did you just say you're going to "get jiggy"? Seriously?
You know nobody says that anymore unless they're being
ironic. It's not cool. Really.

Sally, it doesn't matter what kids are saying these days.
You're having trouble talking to your daughter, right?
How old is she? Yeah. Thirteen. At thirteen, girls are
vicious, especially to their mothers. Look, I'm not a
mother myself, but it's better to be yourself than to try
to "relate" to a teenager and use their language. You just
can't do it. She'll laugh at you. I swear, it's better to be a
regular mom than to try to be the "cool" mom.

If my mother heard me say that, she would die of shock!

THE CUT
seriocomic

CATHERINE

No, I couldn't wear that. It's too . . . low-cut. I guess
I am conservative! I'd feel embarrassed if I wore that. I
wouldn't feel like myself. I'm not saying you look bad or
slutty or anything. This is totally my problem. I'm self-
conscious. I'm just not as confident as you.

That's just it! I do have big boobs. That makes me want
to cover them up, not show them! You would not want to
look like this. You wouldn't. I promise you. There are
things I know, things I see about myself—

I guess everyone is like this about themselves. I wish I
could get over it; I do.

Oh . . . OK. I'll . . . try on the dress. I can't believe I'm
doing this! Don't laugh.

MEETING
seriocomic

TARA

Don't. Please. When he comes, don't be like this, Dad.
Don't play dumb! You know what I mean. Don't ask a
lot of questions. Don't put him on the spot. He's already
feeling nervous, and he wants to impress you. Give him a
break. I really like him.

Oh! And Mom, don't bring out baby pictures or tell embarrassing stories about me. What's embarrassing? I'll
make this easy. Don't tell *any* stories. There will be other
things to talk about! Well, you can tell nice stories. What
does that mean? Use your common sense, Mom. If I was
embarrassed or humiliated, it's off-limits!

Oh, God, he's here! I really hope you like him!

THE MUSE
seriocomic

IANNA

Do you think that guy was really deaf? He was begging for money because he was deaf. Since when does being deaf keep you from getting work? I mean, you can't be a DJ, but there's plenty of things you can do. That's an easy thing to pretend, too. Much easier than pretending to be blind. I swear that my dad pretends to be deaf all the time. Whenever you say something to him when he's watching TV or reading, he's oblivious. It just seems awfully convenient sometimes.

Maybe I should start doing that. I should have done it today. Well, this trip to the post office with you isn't exactly exciting.

Ouch! Don't hit me!

BEST-FRIEND BLUES

seriocomic

FENLON

It's going to be OK. I swear it. You'll get over him. He's not worth it. You're too good for him.

Look, Lindsey, I feel like a broken record. I've been saying all of these things for a month. A month! I *do* feel sorry for you. I understand, I relate, and all of that! But I'm a little sick of always having the same conversations with you. I really want to be your friend right now, someone who's there for you, but I really think we have to work on getting your mind *off* of him now. Why don't we go in here and buy some new music?

Oh, God, Lindsey, don't cry. We'll go somewhere else. I didn't know this was *another* one of the places he took you.

CAT LADY

seriocomic

ZARA

I'm thinking of getting a cat. Does that make me weird? Does that make me a "cat lady"? Because I kind of do want some companionship. Being in an apartment for the first time. I've never had a cat, actually, but I don't think I have the dedication for a dog. Cats take care of themselves for the most part.

Would that bother you? Would you be totally against it? I'm a little lonely, Francie. I don't know anyone here, except you. And you grew up here, so you're always out seeing friends. Which I understand! I don't expect you to hang around here with me.

You're allergic? Oh. OK. Never mind. No, it's fine. I'll be fine. Thanks.

DRIVE BY
seriocomic

ELENA

What should I do? Should I drive away? I can't do that, right? But I can't get in trouble. I can't get a ticket. And if my dad finds out, which he will, I'm dead. Maybe—I know this is wrong, but . . . I'm leaving. No one's looking, right? It's only a scratch. It's hardly anything.

My dad is always going on and on about what a bad driver I am; he'll never let me live this down. Just keep your mouth shut. This is not really a big deal. Just a little tap in a parking lot. A little, itty-bitty dent and a microscopic scratch. That's it. We're leaving. Put your seat belt on. Come on! Quick! I've got to peel out before the owner of this car gets back!

CHECKING
seriocomic

JUNIE

Hi. I'm Junie. So. I'm not really good at this. I don't have radar or anything. Are you gay? Don't get upset. I don't mean anything by it. It's just that I'm gay. And you look really nice. Pretty. And nice. So I was wondering. It's a compliment. Really. You have such a kind face. I bet you'd be really easy to talk to. Are you a good listener? I thought so. I can tell.

It's a shame you're not . . . you know. Maybe we can be friends? Just get to know each other? I promise, I won't make a move or anything. Unless you want me to.

REBOUNDING

seriocomic

TAMARA

This is no good. I hate it! What made me decide to paint the walls red? They look pink, don't they? Hot pink. It's giving me a headache to look at it. I thought once I got it up, it might dry darker or different. It's actually making me hot, and not in a sexy way. I feel like it's a hundred and fifty degrees in here. And I just feel so angry! Is it that I'm upset that I made a bad decision or is it THIS COLOR? I hate myself! I hate everyone! I hate my stupid ex-boyfriend who made me feel like changing my whole life so I have this shitty haircut and these goddamn horrible PINK WALLS!! He is the reason for all the misery and sorrow in the world, especially mine! I hate him, I hate him, I hate him!!!!

I feel so much better now. I think I just needed a good scream.

WATCHED
seriocomic

DANICA

Hi. Um, I'm Danica. Da-ni-ca. With a D. No, a D, like
Daniel. Danica. I'm fine. How are you? Well, good. I'm
glad to hear it. No, I don't come here often. Sometimes. I
come here sometimes. I have a friend in this fraternity.
Could you not lean on the wall behind me? I'm getting a
little claustrophobic. Feeling closed in. Can you just back
up a bit? I can't hear very well in here either, but I don't
like to feel people's breath on me. Yeah. I guess that's my
little "thing." I hate it. Yeah, so . . . Thanks.

You've been watching me? When? Why? Tonight? Oh.
Thanks, I guess. I have to tell you that's kind of a creepy
pick-up line. It makes it sound like you've been stalking
me. You have. You admit that. Well, I think my very big,
muscular friend is trying to get my attention. Excuse me!

SUPERSTAR

seriocomic

MAGGIE

Milla, I don't want any calls to bother me. Oh, and get my manicurist on the phone. She did an absolutely lousy job last time. I need my nails fixed immediately. They're already chipped! And if she can't come in, find someone else. In fact, do find someone who does better work. Who does Christina's nails? Get that person. I want the best. I'm sick and tired of people who can't do their jobs properly.

Milla, where is my little red dress? I have an event tonight. Never mind. I'll go shopping. I don't like that dress anyway.

Where are you going? I have about a thousand more things to tell you. I have needs, Milla, needs!

DRAMATIC
MONOLOGUES

THE GRADE
dramatic

SUSAN

I don't understand my grade. I got a B-. I worked on that scene. We rehearsed a lot! We did! Why do you think we didn't? Well, I just got a little brain freeze. I get nervous. That's the whole thing. This is really hard for me, but I got up and did it anyway. And Jason and I totally rehearsed for hours and hours this week. It's not fair! What do I have to do to get an A in this class? I thought when I signed up for this class that it was supposed to be fun and easy. I'm a straight-A student! I never get a B-. This is unbelievable.

BAD BOYFRIEND
dramatic

MARLA

I really think it's just an act. I don't think he means it. He's just friendly. He's just trying to look cool in front of his friends. He likes me. I know it. I see the way he looks at me. I know what he says when we're together. I just think other girls are jealous of me. I don't blame them. 'Cause he's cute. But I trust Ben. He won't take it too far. We have a good thing going. He knows that. I'm the best thing he's ever had in his life. I'm sure of it. Don't you think so?

THE PLAYER
dramatic

JUSTINE

I don't know what to do. I don't want to ruin things for Marla, but she should know about Ben. He keeps calling me. Whenever we go out, he waits until she goes to the bathroom, then he asks me to dance with him. Well, sure, that would be perfectly innocent if he didn't touch my ass and ask me to go home with him the whole time. I just don't know what to do. I feel like no matter what I do, I'm screwed. If I tell Marla, she's going to be pissed at me. She'll think I'm lying. And if I don't tell her—I have to tell her. He's such a creep!

METABOLIC
dramatic

CLARISSA

Look, I'm just skinny, so leave me alone! Not everyone has metabolism issues or whatever you call it. You're just jealous because I don't gain weight and you do. I have to tell you, I am so damn sick of everyone telling me I'm too skinny. I'm thin. I've always been thin. I'll always be thin. This is who I am. It's such a load of crap, all that Oprah stuff that we're all supposed to love our bodies and accept ourselves as we are, because everyone in the world seems to think that I should be unhappy with how I look. It's such hypocrisy! You need to leave me alone about this. I'm serious. I have absolutely had enough. I cannot be held responsible for what I will do if I ever hear the word *skinny* come out of your mouth again.

THE INCIDENT
dramatic

LAUREN

Cindy, something really scary just happened to me. It's sort of funny, too. I'm trying not to laugh, but I think it's because I'm scared. I don't know. I don't know what to think. It's just so surreal. This guy—outside of the science labs—flashed me. I know it sounds stupid! But there was something so crazy about it. It really scared me. It was, like, broad daylight! And he was just walking toward me. It completely freaked me out. Do you think I should report this? Or will they just laugh at me? But if I don't say anything, maybe—maybe it could be worse for someone else. He was just so gross! I don't know, Cindy, maybe it doesn't make sense, but I'm scared.

FOOT-IN-MOUTH DISEASE
dramatic

REGINA

I'm sorry. I'm sorry. That wasn't funny. I don't know what I was thinking. I'm an idiot. A huge, stupid ass. I didn't think—I wasn't thinking. I didn't know your brother was retarded. Not that it matters. It *not* funny to make fun of retarded people. I'm just a huge pig. Look, I admit it. I make fun of other people so no one makes fun of me. It's really hard for me to say that. And I know it's wrong and I'm wrong and I'm a total jerk. I'm really sorry. I'm so embarrassed. Please forgive me. I'm a complete idiot.

DUMPED

dramatic

JASMINE

Look, I don't hate you anymore. I *thank* you for what you did. You opened my eyes to how horrible people can be. I went away for a weekend—a *weekend*!—and you stole my boyfriend away. Because you knew he was a good guy, unlike any other guys you ever went out with.

I should not blame him! It was your fault. You threw yourself at him. He's a *guy*, what else is he going to do? I mean, I'm mad at him, especially because it was *you*, but I can't blame him for being human. You're the skank here. You ruined everything. But like I said, I'm glad. Now I know I can never trust you. Now I know how awful people can be. Thanks a lot, Alicia.

UNFAIR
dramatic

LOTTIE

Sorry, can I ask you a question? I was just wondering
about something. Why did Hallie get chosen to go to
D.C.? I just want to know what I could have done better.
Because I think I did my best. I think I've worked really
hard all year. I really don't get why I wasn't chosen to
represent the school. I'm also a great ambassador; I'm the
class president. I run the yearbook. I have tons of school
spirit. It just seems unfair to me. It just seems like . . . It
seems like you don't like me. It seems like maybe this decision had nothing to do with schoolwork or our essays.
Because I know mine was better, everyone told me so. I
think I was cheated of this because, for some reason, you
have something against me.

I'm not being combative; I just want to know. I think I
deserve to know, actually.

SEA CHANGE
dramatic

BRENDA

Where would you most like to live? Not like that. I mean, what would it look like? Would you want to live in the mountains or the woods or the beach? I'm so sick of fields. I can't decide what kind of place I want to be in, but I know it's not this. I've never even been on vacation outside of Nebraska. I know I sound like a complete stereotype, but the minute I graduate I'm outta here. I don't know where I'm going, but I am going. To be honest, the whole idea scares me. I think about going to New York, but that's terrifying. I might at least start out smaller. I'm thinking the beach. I'm dying to see what the ocean's like, Carol.

Yeah! Come with me! That would be so fun—you, me, and a million miles of sand. Let's do it, Carol. I'm not kidding. I just have to make a change.

TEACHER
dramatic

CHRISTINE

There's this little girl in my class who reminds me of me
when I was a kid. She's little, and she likes stories. Cute.
When I was little I didn't think I was cute. And this
girl . . . doesn't have friends. The other kids don't play
with her. I don't know why. She's sweet. She's just shy.
I wish I could do something to help her. I wish someone
did something to help me. I don't think any child should
feel all alone. I was so sad when I was little.

Am I getting too involved? Personalizing too much? I
wanted to be a kindergarten teacher because I love kids.
I just didn't think they'd affect me so much. I just love
these kids so much.

JUDGMENT
dramatic

BECCA

Why shouldn't I eat this? Just because I have a few extra pounds doesn't mean I can't enjoy ice cream every once in a while. You know, I've been holding back for the past few weeks. To see if we're just hitting a rough patch. To see if this would pass. But the fact is, Mike, I don't like you anymore. You're too critical. You pick at me all the time. I've tried ignoring it, laughing it off, making fun of you to show you how it feels, but the fact is, you're not a very nice person. I guess you're one of those guys that's nice until he actually "has" you. You used to be romantic and charming and complimentary.

I'm not overreacting. Maybe I do need to lose a little weight, but that's for me to decide, not you. Oh, by the way, you're paying for my ice cream. I deserve at least that for putting up with you over the last few weeks.

OBJECT OF AFFECTION
dramatic

LEELEE

I am going to sound so conceited right now. I really don't mean this how it sounds. I . . . feel sorry for Mark. He likes me so much, and I'm just not that interested. But I almost want to say yes since he likes me so much. I don't think I've ever known anyone who liked me so much. It makes me feel like I *ought* to date him. What if I never meet anyone who worships me like him? What if he's the best I can do in that department? It seems so unfair that the one person in my whole life so far who's crazy about me is a guy that I feel nothing for. Sure, I like him. He's nice. But he does nothing for me.

What should I do?

GOING
dramatic

WIN

What's wrong with joining the Peace Corps? What could be better? You should be proud of me. I want to make a difference in the world. There are so many people who need help, and I'm in a position to do something about it. It's not dangerous! Thousands and thousands of people do this. It's not like I'm going to walk around the jungle late at night. I'm going to be teaching.

I don't actually need your permission to do this. I told you because I thought you'd be proud of me. Maybe even excited about it. I am! I can't wait to go. I couldn't be happier. Can't you at least pretend to be happy about this? Once I go, I'm not going to see you for a long time. I don't want to leave things like this.

THE EMPLOYEE
dramatic

GRACE

I can't stand my boss. He talks to me as if I'm stupid. And he always has a smirk on his face. I swear he thinks he owns me. Like I'm his possession. Like having a young secretary makes him manly or something. I started wearing turtlenecks because I thought he was looking down my shirt all the time. He was always hanging over me. I can't sue him; I have no proof. But he just makes my skin crawl. I just can't get over the feeling that I'm better than my job. I could do my boss's job. It's not that hard. He's mostly full of crap and spends a lot of time trying to look busy and important.

The worst part is, maybe my parents were right. Maybe I should have gone to college. Now it seems too late.

RENT

dramatic

MARLEEN

Mr. Ianucci, I need to talk to you. I just started a new job, and I haven't gotten a paycheck yet. But it's coming. See, I thought I would get it after two weeks, but it turns out that I have to wait a month until my first paycheck. So I don't have my rent money. Yet. I'll have it by next Thursday. I swear. Is that OK?

It's not? Well, what am I supposed to do? I paid you all the money I had in the world for the down payment and my first month's rent here. Actually, I maxed out my credit card between you and groceries, buying a futon— We're talking about a week. You're going to get your money. It's the best I can do! Please, please, you have to give me a break! This will never, ever happen again. Please let me do this just this once; please!

EDUCATION
dramatic

ANGELA

I'm not black. I'm Dominican. Yeah, there's a difference.
Black people are from Africa. Dominican people are from
the Dominican Republic. That's in the Caribbean,
dummy. Dominican people speak Spanish. Just because I
look black to you doesn't mean I am. Look, you need to
stop being ignorant. I am trying to educate you. I'm not
black. I have black hair, I have dark skin, but I am *not
black*. I have a whole different culture.

What if I told you that you look like white trash? You
might not be, but that's what you look like to me. Look,
don't dish it out if you can't take it.

HOMEBODY

dramatic

DANI

No, thanks. I'm just not a party person. I'm a homebody.

Thanks for pointing that out. No, I don't have many dates. In fact, I don't have any dates. I don't get a lot of attention, and the attention I get, I don't want. Maybe I do need to get out more, but I'm not about to go to a party where I don't know anybody. I'd feel awkward. Thanks for asking, though. Have a good time.

Look, you're really nice. I can tell you feel sorry for me, but I'm really OK. I'm focused on other things. I'll be fine here at home. Have a great time.

DARK
dramatic

VIRGINIA

It's been dark for so long. I feel like I haven't seen the sun for weeks. I'm so tired.

Can I tell you something? Promise you won't act weird around me? No. Never mind. It's nothing. I just feel like . . .

I'm just really sad. And nothing seems to be working out for me lately. I don't know what to do. When I think about the future, it's just so . . . bleak. And I feel like . . . I don't know what to do. I feel kind of hopeless. And I just want—I want to feel better. I want to—There's just no point to me living. I mean really, logically, when you think about it, there's really no point to me. I just want to sleep forever.

THE DIRECTOR
dramatic

RORY

Are you saying what I think you're saying? You'll give me the part if I—what? This really happens? I really thought the casting couch was extinct. That this didn't really happen anymore. Do I give off a slutty vibe? Does this really work? Yes, I want a career. I *really* want a career. But here's the thing. I have *talent*.

Don't laugh! I do. This is not the way business is done in this town. I don't believe that. I just don't believe that every actress has slept her way to the top. Even if they did, it doesn't mean that I have to. I'm going to prove you wrong. No, you won't see me again. On the big screen maybe, but not in person. And certainly not in your bed.

STYLE
dramatic

LIZ

Mom, I am not trying to act black. I am aware that I am white. There is no way I could be unaware with that fact. This is how people dress at school. Everybody. Black and white. Besides, there shouldn't be these boundaries and judgments—this is white; that is black. We should all be whatever we want.

You are being so narrow-minded. I am not going to change my clothes. This is how I dress. This is an expression of my personality. I bought these clothes with the money from my birthday. It's *my* money. It was given to me. I'm old enough to make my own choices. Face it, Mom, I'm an adult now.

THE CHOICE
dramatic

HOPE

This is what I don't understand. I want to be a musician. I do. I practice all the time. But there's always someone who's there in the practice rooms when I arrive, and still there when I leave. So there's always someone who's working harder, who wants it more. Is there any hope for me? Be honest. I really want to know, Mr. Hopper. I want to be a professional musician, but if I really can't possibly make it, I'd rather know it now than find out five years down the line. I can't even imagine what else I'd do, but there's got to be something else I can do for a living. Maybe I'll just play for fun and do some boring job for money. I don't know. It sounds horrible, but if that's the reality of it, if I'll never be good enough, just let me know.

IN-LAW
dramatic

EMILY

Your mother. She's around all the time. Don't you think you spend a lot of time with your mother for an adult? I'm not saying I don't like her. I like her a lot. She's very kind, and she really loves you. But don't you want to move out of her house? Do you think there will ever be a time when you'd want to move out of her house? Wouldn't you like to have your own place where we could be alone together? Like adults? Are you catching my drift?

So you're just saying you want to spend the rest of your life living like a baby with your mother cooking for you, cleaning for you, giving you baths—Well, I just assumed! She does everything else for you! I have to tell you, at first I thought it was sweet that you got along so well with your mother. Now, I think it's sick. Really, Justin, it's perverted.

THE BOSS
dramatic

PETRA

It's very flattering, but—Really, I wish you'd stop that. I didn't want to say this right out, I was hoping you'd take the hint, but . . . I don't like you. I work for you. But I'm not interested in dating you. You're my boss. You're a lot older than me.

That does not make me a lesbian. Or frigid. Or scared of your manliness. I'm just not interested. Is that all right? Can I just go on working here without having you hit on me, please? I really didn't want to say this—

OK, you don't have to be insulting. I'm trying to be nice. Now I'm ugly. Thanks a lot. I'm—I'm—going on break now. Excuse me.

CHRISTMAS BREAK
dramatic

HARRIET

Gia, I'd like to take a walk. Alone. I need some time to think. Can you understand that? I know I'm hardly home anymore. But I just need a few minutes to myself. I do miss you when I'm away. You're my little sister. But even though I love you, sometimes I just need time away from you. Away from everybody, not just you. There isn't a single person in the world I want to be around *all* the time.

Tell you what. Let's go out later and get some ice cream. Just you and me. What do you say? I want to hear all about school and your friends. OK, little bug? Promise I'll be back soon. Then we'll have fun the whole rest of the day. Promise.

FIRE
dramatic

SHANNON

Wake up, Viv! The fire alarm is going off! It smells like smoke. I *know* the fire alarms are never anything real, but I really smell smoke. This one might be for real. Come on! What if it is real just this once? It will be my fault if you burn to death, and your parents will blame me for your death! I'm not being dramatic. I'm being . . . concerned!

Come on! Put on some pants and slippers and let's go! We don't have time to argue. Vivi, I will drag you out of here if I have to. Don't go back to sleep! Don't! Vivi, you're right, I can't drag you down three floors. Please, let's go. Hurry! Please. I'm going to have to leave without you. I don't want to. Don't make me, please?

THE BREAKUP
dramatic

NOELLE

Why are you breaking up with me? What did I do? Was I a bad girlfriend? If I was, you should have told me! Was I not pretty enough or not smart enough or not enough fun? What is it then, Jack? There has to be a reason. Don't pull that "it's not you, it's me" thing! Everybody knows that means it's not you; it's me. I thought everything was good! Whatever was wrong, I can fix it. Is there someone else? Tell me the truth.

I can't believe this is happening. I didn't know this was coming. How could I not know? Why didn't you tell me? This is so unfair. You're breaking my heart; you know that? I really thought—I felt—Jack, won't you reconsider? I promise I'll do better. Give me another chance!

THE HOSPITAL
dramatic

SAMANTHA

Surgery? *(Beat.)* Is that really necessary? What happens if I don't get the surgery? So I have to. I have to, basically, or I'll die. How did this happen? Can the surgery go wrong? Will I have a huge scar? Can this happen again?

I just moved here. There's no one here who can take care of me. I can't pay the hospital bill, either. I don't have insurance. Why is this happening to me? Is there any, *any* way around this? Will this have any lasting effects on me? Will I be able to . . . have kids someday? God, I never thought I wanted any, but I always thought it was a possibility if I changed my mind. I can't believe God would take that choice away from me. This is too much right now. This is a lot to take in. Can I have a moment by myself?

No, there's no one you can call. I'm pretty much on my own.

CAUGHT
dramatic

ROXIE

I didn't cheat. I swear to you I didn't. Annika is lying. She didn't see anything. I wouldn't do that! Look, I don't need a black mark on my academic record. I wouldn't risk getting caught. I'm not a cheater! I get good grades. I study!

Don't do this. Those people who say they saw me are wrong. I'm not lying. This is the truth.

(Beat.) You don't know what it's like. I work so hard. And I've been so busy. I try to do everything—get A's in school, do extracurricular activities and community service—and it's exhausting. Everything is riding on me not only getting into a great college, but also getting a scholarship. I'll be the first person in my family to go to college. This is huge. And I've worked for it. I've worked for it so hard. I did one thing wrong. One little thing! I've been under so much pressure. Can't we just forget this happened? It will never happen again. I just need one more chance . . .

THE AUTHOR

Kristen Dabrowski is an actress, writer, acting teacher, and director. She received her M.F.A. from The Oxford School of Drama in Oxford, England. The actor's life has taken her all over the United States and England. Her other books, published by Smith and Kraus, Inc., include *111 Monologues for Middle School Actors Volume 1, The Ultimate Audition Book for Teens 3,* the *10+* play series, the *Teens Speak* series, and *20 Ten-Minute Plays for Teens.* Currently, she lives in the world's smallest apartment in New York City. You can contact the author at monologuemadness@yahoo.com.